D1224327

The Negro Leagues' Integration Era

By Bo Smolka

Content Consultant
Raymond Doswell, Ed.D.
Curator, Negro Leagues Baseball Museum

Printed in the United States of America,
North Mankato, Minnesota
052012
092012

 THIS BOOK CONTAINS AT LEAST 10% RECYCLED MATERIALS.

Editor: Chrös McDougall
Series Designer: Emily Love

Photo Credits
Negro Leagues Baseball Museum, cover, 1, 20, 60; AP Images, 7, 9, 11, 18, 26, 38; Bettmann/Corbis/AP Images, 15, 35, 36, 41, 45, 49, 55; Mark Rucker/Transcendental Graphics, Getty Images, 23, 50; John J. Lent/AP Images, 25; Jack Harris/AP Images, 30; Dan Grossi/AP Images, 32; Harry Harris/AP Images, 42, 53; Jacob Harris/AP Images, 57

Design elements: Patricia Hofmeester/Shutterstock Images; Bryan Solomon/ Shutterstock Images

Library of Congress Cataloging-in-Publication Data
Smolka, Bo, 1965-
  The Negro leagues' integration era / Bo Smolka.
     p. cm. -- (The Negro baseball leagues)
  Includes bibliographical references.
  ISBN 978-1-61783-509-4
  1. Negro leagues--History--Juvenile literature. 2. African American baseball players--History--Juvenile literature. 3. Discrimination in sports--United States--History--Juvenile literature. I. Title.
  GV875.N35S66 2012
  796.357'64--dc23
                          2012010836

TABLE OF CONTENTS

A GAME OF BLACK AND WHITE

Jackie Robinson stood in the batter's box, wearing a crisp Montreal Royals uniform. He dug in his cleats, took a practice swing, and looked out toward pitcher Warren Sandell. A crowd of 52,000—twice the capacity—had crammed into the ballpark in Jersey City, New Jersey. They were there to see the home team face the Royals in the International League season opener.

Many in the crowd thought this day would never come. Jackie Robinson, a black man, was playing in a game in baseball's minor leagues. It was April 18, 1946. No black player had suited up in the major or minor leagues since the late 1800s. In the third inning, with two men on base, Sandell delivered a letter-high fastball. Robinson took a big swing. *Crack!* The ball sailed deep over the left-field fence for a three-run home run.

The crowd went wild. Blacks and whites cheered together. Teammates from the North and from the South congratulated Robinson. Robinson and other black players would still face fierce opposition for years to come. The journey for the sport to be fully integrated was only just beginning. But for the first time, baseball could truly be called the national pastime.

WHAT A START!

Jackie Robinson did more than hit a three-run home run in his first game with Montreal. He also had three other hits, including two bunt singles. He also stole two bases and scored four runs. Montreal won, 14–1. One sportswriter covering the game wrote that Robinson "did everything but help the ushers seat the crowd."

A HISTORY OF DISCRIMINATION

Since the late 1880s, blacks had not been allowed in what was known as "organized baseball." That included major league teams and all the minor league teams associated with them. The United States was a very divided country then. In many places, especially in the South, blacks faced discrimination and hatred every day. Blacks could not stay in the same hotels as whites. They could not go to the same schools or restaurants. This separation included baseball. No organized white baseball teams would sign black players. The best white players were in the major leagues. The best blacks played in the Negro Leagues. This came to be known as baseball's color line.

By the 1940s, more and more people were asking why blacks were not allowed to play Major League Baseball (MLB). One of them was Brooklyn Dodgers president Branch Rickey.

ROBINSON IN THE NEGRO LEAGUES

Jackie Robinson made no secret of the fact that he did not like life in the Negro Leagues. He described his one season with the Kansas City Monarchs as "a pretty miserable way to make a buck." After he had signed with the Dodgers, Robinson wrote a magazine article that detailed life in the Negro Leagues. He wrote that the bus trips were long and uncomfortable, good food was hard to find, and hotels where Negro Leagues teams stayed were "usually of the cheapest kind. The rooms are dingy and dirty." He also complained about "sloppy umpiring." Negro Leagues owners were angry at Robinson. Effa Manley, owner of the Newark Eagles, said, "Jackie Robinson is where he is today because of organized Negro baseball."

Jackie Robinson signs a contract with the Brooklyn Dodgers' Montreal farm team in 1945. Dodgers president Branch Rickey is in black.

He had scouts check out the Negro Leagues. He wanted to find a young, talented player for what became known as Rickey's "great experiment." He wanted to see whether a black man could succeed in the major leagues. Dodgers scouts, and some black sportswriters who followed the Negro Leagues closely, thought they had the perfect candidate to integrate baseball: Jackie Robinson.

JACKIE ROBINSON

MULTISPORT STAR

Jackie Robinson was a four-sport star at UCLA. Not only did he excel in baseball, but he was the conference scoring leader in basketball, a college champion in track and field, and a top running back in football. The baseball team at UCLA now plays its home games at Jackie Robinson Stadium.

Jack Roosevelt Robinson was born in 1919 in Georgia. His mother moved Jackie and his siblings to California when he was young. They grew up poor. From a young age, Robinson had to endure insults and taunts. Sometimes he ignored them.

Sometimes he did not. One time he got in a rock-throwing battle with a white neighbor. The white man's daughter had said mean things to Robinson.

Robinson was a star multisport athlete at the University of California, Los Angeles (UCLA) and later joined the army. One day, he was riding an army bus. He was told he needed to go to

Jackie Robinson was a star football player at UCLA. He also competed in baseball, basketball, and track and field for the Bruins.

the back of the bus because he was black. He refused. He knew that army rules allowed him to sit wherever he liked in that bus. Robinson left the army not long afterward.

Robinson then joined the Kansas City Monarchs. They were one of the top teams in the Negro Leagues. The Monarchs had been in the Negro National League (NNL), but they were in the Negro American League (NAL) when Robinson played. Robinson hit .345 for the Monarchs and was named an all-star shortstop.

Rickey probably thought it was unfair that blacks were not allowed to play in MLB. But Rickey also knew that Negro Leagues games were drawing big crowds. He probably figured that if the Dodgers signed a black player, many of those fans would buy tickets to Dodgers games.

On August 28, 1945, Rickey called Robinson to his office for a meeting. Robinson thought he was being invited to join a Negro Leagues team. But then Rickey said to him, "I'm interested in you as a candidate for the Brooklyn National League club. I think you can play in the major leagues."

Rickey warned Robinson that being the first black player in the major leagues would be incredibly hard. Fans would taunt him. Opposing players would try to hit him with pitches or hurt him while running the bases. People would yell awful

Jackie Robinson crosses home plate after hitting a three-run home run for Montreal in the first game of the 1946 season.

things at his wife. Rickey made clear that Robinson would have to do his best to ignore all of that.

"I'm looking for a ballplayer with guts enough not to fight back," Rickey said.

Robinson told Rickey he could be that player. Rickey signed Robinson to a contract. In October 1945, Rickey announced that Robinson would be joining the Dodgers' top minor league team in Montreal, Canada. This was front-page news around the United States. Blacks were thrilled that the color line would be broken.

Some Negro Leaguers, though, did not think Robinson was a good choice. Robinson had only played one season in the Negro Leagues. There were other, more accomplished Negro League players such as pitcher Leroy "Satchel" Paige, outfielder James "Cool Papa" Bell, and first baseman Walter "Buck" Leonard. A lot of people thought one of those players deserved to be the first to cross the color

MONTREAL

Montreal was a great choice for Jackie Robinson's first stop in organized baseball. In Canada, Robinson experienced little of the racial discrimination he faced in the United States. "The people of Montreal were warm and wonderful to us," he recalled years later.

line. But by 1945, Paige was 39 years old. Bell was 42. Leonard was 38. Rickey wanted a younger player. There were other talented young black players. But Rickey wanted Robinson.

In early 1946, Robinson reported to Florida for spring training. Because he was black, Robinson was not allowed to stay at the same hotel as his Montreal teammates. When he rode a bus, he had to sit in the back. Even Montreal's manager, Clay Hopper, who was from Mississippi, begged the Dodgers not to put Robinson on his team.

On the field, though, there was no holding Robinson back. He quickly established a reputation as a great hitter and quick, daring base runner. Once he reached base, Robinson would take his lead. Bouncing on his toes, he might fake like he was stealing a base to distract the pitcher. Or he would go, bursting like a flash toward the next base.

NO BLACKS ALLOWED HERE

In one spring training game in 1946 in Sanford, Florida, Jackie Robinson got a hit, stole a base, and later slid home with a run. When he got to his feet, the local sheriff was standing there. He announced the game was over. According to a local law at the time, blacks and whites were not allowed to share a field.

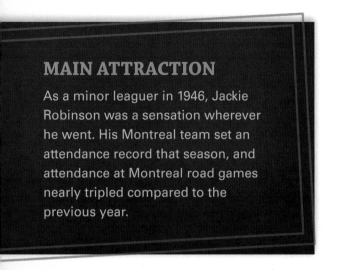

MAIN ATTRACTION

As a minor leaguer in 1946, Jackie Robinson was a sensation wherever he went. His Montreal team set an attendance record that season, and attendance at Montreal road games nearly tripled compared to the previous year.

This was how he had played the game in the Negro Leagues. Robinson batted .349 for Montreal in 1946 and stole 40 bases. His team won the league championship.

At the end of the season, Hopper, the manager who had not wanted Robinson on his team, shook his hand. "You're a great ballplayer and a fine gentleman," Hopper said. "It's been wonderful having you on the team."

The next spring, Rickey announced that Robinson was being promoted to the Brooklyn Dodgers. The "great experiment" was about to begin. And with it came the beginning of the end for the Negro Leagues.

In Montreal, Jackie Robinson experienced little of the racial discrimination he faced in the United States.

CALLS TO INTEGRATE

Long before Jackie Robinson came along, blacks and whites played baseball with one another. In 1884, a catcher named Moses "Fleetwood" Walker played for Toledo in the American Association. That was considered a major league at the time. Walker is considered to have been the first black major league player.

But within a few years, blacks had been effectively banned from organized baseball. In 1887, the New York Giants planned to have a black pitcher named George Stovey pitch against the Chicago White Stockings in an exhibition game. The White Stockings' player/manager, Adrian "Cap" Anson, furiously objected. He said his team would not take the field if Stovey or any other blacks played.

Led by Anson and others, there was soon a firm color line in baseball. There was nothing in writing, but it was understood that no teams in organized baseball would sign black players.

The top black players such as Oscar Charleston and James "Cool Papa" Bell joined all-black teams that formed in cities such as Chicago, Philadelphia, and Pittsburgh. These cities had large black populations. By the 1920s, the Negro Leagues had formed. The biggest Negro Leagues were the NNL and the NAL. Negro Leagues teams often played major

DRAWING THE COLOR LINE

Adrian "Cap" Anson is considered one of the finest first basemen in baseball history. He played in the majors in the late 1800s and hit better than .300 19 times in a 22-year career. He was also a top manager, leading his team to five pennants. He was inducted into the National Baseball Hall of Fame in 1939. But he also was steadfastly opposed to blacks in MLB. He is viewed as a major reason the so-called color line came to exist by 1900.

league all-star teams in the off-season, and the Negro Leaguers often won.

To many people, this was a sign that black players were good enough to play in MLB with teams such as the New York Yankees and Chicago Cubs. Newspapers that catered to blacks, such as the *Pittsburgh Courier*, began demanding that black players have that chance. In many places, blacks were being admitted to parks and beaches and swimming pools that had

CUBANS

One of the great oddities of early American baseball is that light-skinned Cubans were permitted to play in the majors, but darker-skinned Americans were not. In 1902, Cuban Chick Pedroes played briefly for the Chicago Cubs. Then, in 1911, the Cincinnati Reds signed two Cuban players, Rafael Almeida and Armando Marsans. They became the first Latin American major leaguers of the twentieth century. The Reds touted the two players as "pure Spaniards, without a trace of colored blood." Overall, more than 30 light-skinned Cubans played in the majors before Jackie Robinson. Darker-skinned Cubans, such as Martin Dihigo, were relegated to the Negro Leagues.

Longtime Negro Leagues outfielder Oscar Charleston was later inducted into the National Baseball Hall of Fame, but he never had an opportunity to play in the major leagues.

been off-limits before. If those places can be integrated, they wrote, why can't baseball?

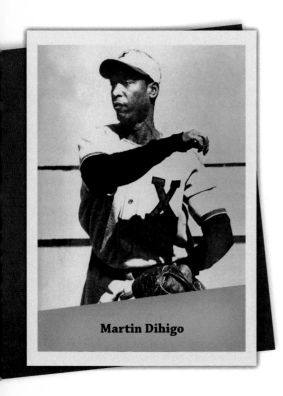

Martin Dihigo

Wendell Smith of the *Pittsburgh Courier* called on fans to demand integration. "The final blow to be struck in this long-waged war for Negroes in the majors remains to be struck by the fans," Smith wrote in 1942. "An army of baseball fans from coast to coast must rise and fire the final shot demanding that the owners hire Negro players."

Despite this pressure, MLB owners were in no hurry to integrate baseball. One reason was money. Many major league teams rented out their stadiums to local Negro Leagues teams. If blacks joined the majors, they thought, the Negro Leagues might end. All that rent money would be gone.

Some in the Negro Leagues opposed integration as well. They, too, worried that if the top black players joined the major leagues, the Negro Leagues would fold. Vic Harris, a player/manager for the Homestead Grays, said that integration would help the top black players. But, he asked, "how could the other 75-80 percent survive?"

In 1939, the *Pittsburgh Courier*'s Smith interviewed many major league players and managers about having blacks in organized baseball. "I would certainly use a [black] player who had the ability," Pirates manager Pie Traynor said. But he never did, and he never appeared to try.

One big reason for Traynor's inaction might have been the baseball commissioner at the time, Kenesaw Mountain Landis. He did not want blacks in the major leagues. At one point, he canceled games between a team of MLB all-stars and a team of Negro Leaguers. When Negro Leagues executive Andrew "Rube" Foster asked Landis about this, Landis reportedly said, "Mr. Foster, when you beat our teams it gives us a black eye."

> **"If Kenesaw Mountain Landis had lived another 20 years, you never would have seen me or Jackie in baseball."**
>
> *—Don Newcombe, a black star for the Dodgers, Cincinnati Reds, and Cleveland Indians from 1949 to 1960*

Josh Gibson and Walter "Buck" Leonard also received a long look from the Washington Senators of the American League (AL). During the 1930s and 1940s, their team, the Homestead Grays, played many of its home games at the

Senators' stadium. Senators owner Clark Griffith had seen them play many times. He had seen Gibson crush balls into the deepest reaches of the ballpark. One day after a game, Griffith met with Gibson and Leonard. Griffith asked them if they thought they were good enough to play in the major leagues. The players said they would love to find out. But they never got the chance.

"The reason we haven't got you colored baseball players on the team," Griffith told them, "is that the time hasn't come."

At about that time, Leo Durocher, the Brooklyn Dodgers' manager, complained that Landis was the main obstacle to blacks in organized baseball. Landis was furious. He argued

"HE'S THE WRONG COLOR"

In 1945, a Boston politician demanded that if the Red Sox wanted to continue to play baseball at home on Sundays, they must offer tryouts to black players. So three players, including Jackie Robinson, went for a tryout. By all accounts, Robinson had a great day. He pounded balls off Fenway Park's famous Green Monster. He slammed balls over it. Red Sox players crowded the dugout to watch. Red Sox scout Hugh Duffy, who was watching, reportedly said, "What a ballplayer! Too bad he's the wrong color." It became clear that the tryout was a sham, done only to satisfy the politician. The Red Sox did not have any interest in signing any of the players. In fact, the Red Sox were the last major league team to integrate.

The 1942 Homestead Grays

that there was no rule that kept blacks out of the game. Many people knew otherwise. There was clearly an unwritten agreement among the owners. And it had Landis's blessing. Landis died in 1944. Many people believe, had Landis still been alive in 1947, Jackie Robinson would not have joined the Dodgers that year.

By September 1945, World War II was over and thousands of blacks in the army returned home. The momentum to integrate baseball grew. Albert "Happy" Chandler, who took over as baseball commissioner after Landis died, seemed much more open to having blacks in the majors. If blacks could serve in the US Army and die in war, Chandler said, then they should be able to play in MLB.

The time, it seemed, had finally come.

THE "GREAT EXPERIMENT"

In one season in the minor leagues, Jackie Robinson hit .349 and led his team to the league championship. He had shown he was ready for the major leagues. But the major leagues still did not seem ready for him.

In 1946, a committee of baseball executives held a special meeting. One of the topics was "the Race Question." The group concluded that black players did not have the ability to play in MLB. They also said that if blacks joined the majors, more black fans would attend the games. This might keep white fans away. The committee's conclusion seemed clear: Blacks did not belong in the major leagues.

After Robinson's great 1946 season with Montreal, there was word he might be promoted to the majors in 1947. Some Dodgers planned to refuse to play if Robinson was on the team. Dodgers' general manager Branch Rickey called in the players and quickly squashed that plan.

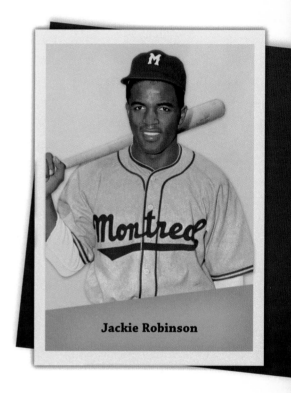

Jackie Robinson

Robinson began spring training in 1947 with Montreal. Montreal and the Dodgers held spring training in Cuba that season. The teams played seven exhibition games against each other. Rickey thought this was a good chance to see whether Robinson could play against major leaguers. He got his answer. Robinson hit .625 in the seven games and stole seven bases. On April 9, Rickey announced that Robinson would start the regular season with the Brooklyn Dodgers.

Jackie Robinson stands with Brooklyn Dodgers teammates, *from left*, John "Spider" Jorgensen, Harold "Pee Wee" Reese, and Ed Stanky before the 1947 season opener.

"This is your big chance," Clay Hopper, Robinson's manager with Montreal, told him. "Now go out there and make good."

It is hard to imagine the pressure Robinson felt. "If he had failed, it might have been another 50 years before [another black player got the chance in the majors]," said former Negro Leagues star John "Buck" O'Neil.

In Robinson's first official MLB at-bat on April 15, 1947, he grounded out to third. Later in the game, though, Robinson laid down a bunt and reached first base on an error. He then scored on a double, which proved to be the winning run in a 5–3 Dodgers win. In his first road game, Robinson and the Dodgers traveled across town to face the New York Giants. Nearly 40,000 people packed the Polo Grounds. In the third inning, Robinson swung at a high, inside pitch and drilled a line drive off the scoreboard in left field for his first major league home run. The next day,

OPENING DAY

When the Brooklyn Dodgers took the field for Opening Day on April 15, 1947, the crowd was about 27,000. That was 2,000 fewer than Opening Day the year before, and 5,000 fewer than the ballpark's capacity. It is estimated that less than half the crowd was white. It appeared that some white fans were not yet ready to share the stadium with black fans. By the end of the season, though, the Dodgers had drawn 1.8 million fans, a team record.

more than 52,000 people crammed into the Polo Grounds. That was the biggest Saturday crowd ever at the ballpark. Robinson put on a show. He went 3-for-4 with two singles and a double. By the end of his first week, Robinson was hitting .429.

STANDING TALL

As Rickey had predicted, bigotry and hatred followed Robinson everywhere. Early in the season, the Dodgers were playing a series against the Philadelphia Phillies. "Why don't you go back to the cotton fields where you belong?" one person yelled. "They're waiting for you in the jungles, black boy!" hollered another. These taunts—and even meaner ones—were not coming from fans. They were coming from the Phillies and their manager, an Alabama-born man named Ben Chapman.

"This day, of all the unpleasant days in my life, brought me nearer to cracking up than I had ever been," Robinson later wrote. Robinson almost charged into the Phillies dugout. Then he remembered what Rickey had said: *I'm looking for a ballplayer with guts enough not to fight back.*

> **"Jackie Robinson gave all of us—not only black athletes, but every black person in this country—a sense of our own strength."**
>
> —*Former Negro Leagues player and MLB great Hank Aaron*

28

With the score 0–0 in the eighth inning, Robinson singled. He then stole second and later scored. The Dodgers won, 1–0.

The taunting from the Phillies went on for three games. Then one of Robinson's teammates, Ed Stanky, stuck up for Robinson. He told the Phillies to leave Robinson alone. So did others. Robinson finally began to feel like part of the team.

Later that season, the Dodgers were playing the St. Louis Cardinals. St. Louis outfielder Enos Slaughter hit a grounder. As he ran toward first base, where Robinson was playing, he drove his metal cleats into Robinson's leg. As Robinson hopped around in pain, his teammates rushed out to his defense. As with the Phillies' incident, the Dodgers rallied around Robinson.

The problems were hardly limited to the field. The Dodgers received hate mail directed at Robinson almost every day.

BROOKLYN'S FINEST

Jackie Robinson played 10 seasons in the major leagues, all with the Brooklyn Dodgers. He finished his career with a lifetime batting average of .311. He hit 137 career home runs and had 197 stolen bases. He was a six-time All-Star and entered the National Baseball Hall of Fame in 1962.

Jackie Robinson attempts to steal home during a 1948 game against the Boston Braves.

People threatened to kill him. People threatened to hurt his wife. People threatened to kidnap his child.

In some cities, Robinson could not stay at the same hotel as his teammates. In Cincinnati, Robinson was allowed to stay at the team hotel, as long as he did not eat in the restaurant or use the pool.

After his strong start, Robinson struggled. On May 1, he was hitting just .225. Some people thought he should be sent back to the minor leagues. Robinson worried that if he were sent back to Montreal, all the critics who thought blacks were not good enough for the majors would be proved right.

His manager, Burt Shotton, kept him in the lineup. That move paid off. On June 5, he went 3-for-4 with a home run and a stolen base. A few days later, he was 4-for-4 with a double and a triple to raise his average to .301. The Dodgers were drawing big crowds. Around the country, fans, especially blacks, eagerly grabbed newspapers to read the latest news about Robinson. With Robinson hitting and running wild on the bases, the Dodgers roared past the Boston Braves and St. Louis Cardinals. They finished the season with a record of 94–60 and won the National League (NL) pennant.

STEALING HOME

One of Jackie Robinson's trademark plays as a base runner was to dance off third base, and try to distract the pitcher. Sometimes, he would sprint for home when the pitcher was in his windup. Robinson stole home 19 times in his career.

Jackie Robinson poses with his Brooklyn Dodgers teammate Harold "Pee Wee" Reese in 1952.

In his first season, Robinson hit .297 with 12 home runs and a league-best 29 stolen bases. He was hit by nine pitches and thrown at countless other times. True to his word, he never fought back. When the season ended, he was named the first winner of the MLB's Rookie of the Year Award.

The Dodgers lost the World Series to the New York Yankees, but by the end of the season, Jackie Robinson had won something more important: respect. Through his courage and his ability, he had changed the face—and the color—of baseball forever.

PEE WEE REESE

Harold "Pee Wee" Reese was the Brooklyn Dodgers' shortstop when Jackie Robinson joined the team. One day, some opposing players began to heckle Reese, who was from Kentucky, about playing with a black man. Reese said nothing. Instead, he walked over to Robinson, put his hand on his shoulder, and began talking to him. The jeering stopped.

With this move, Reese was saying clearly that Robinson was his teammate, and it was about time people started accepting that. "His words weren't important," Robinson would say later. "I don't even remember what he said. It was the gesture of comradeship and support that counted." The scene is now memorialized in a statue at a minor league ballpark in Brooklyn.

4

AFTER JACKIE

By any measure, Branch Rickey's "great experiment" was a great success in 1947. Jackie Robinson had led the Brooklyn Dodgers to the World Series. The Dodgers' turnstiles were spinning at record numbers. Virtually every black baseball fan in the United States was a Dodgers fan. It did not take long for another owner to realize that Rickey was on to something.

Bill Veeck had taken over the Cleveland Indians before the 1947 season. A few years earlier, Veeck had attempted to buy the

Philadelphia Phillies. He claimed his plan had been to add Negro Leagues stars to that team, but the deal never happened. That story is disputed, however. But once Veeck saw the Dodgers' success with Robinson, he moved quickly. He sent scouts out to watch top Negro Leagues talent. Larry Doby, an infielder with the Newark Eagles, was hitting over .400 and leading the NNL in home runs. Veeck signed Doby, and Doby reported to the Indians on July 5, 1947. Eleven weeks after Robinson broke the color line, Doby became the first black player in the AL.

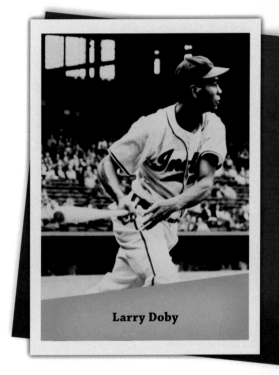

Larry Doby

When Doby walked into the Cleveland clubhouse for the first time, he was greeted with silence. Several of his new teammates refused to shake his hand. When he took the field to warm up for the first time, for several minutes no teammate would play catch with him. That first season, Doby faced all the taunts, insults, and struggles that Robinson did, but he did not have the success.

LARRY DOBY

Larry Doby has always been a footnote in baseball history as the second black player in the modern major leagues. Doby was also the second black manager in the majors. He served as manager of the Chicago White Sox for part of the 1978 season. Frank Robinson was the majors' first black manager when he took over the Cleveland Indians in 1975. Doby did achieve a notable first, though: in 1948, he and Leroy "Satchel" Paige became the first black players to win the World Series.

While Robinson was running wild with Brooklyn, Doby was pretty much sitting on the end of the bench, alone, for Cleveland. In 29 games he hit just .156.

"The only difference [was] that Jackie got all the publicity," Doby said. "You didn't hear much about what I was going through because the media didn't want to repeat the same story."

Doby persevered, though. In 1948, he hit .301 with 14 home runs and led the Indians to the World Series title. Doby played 13 seasons in the major leagues and was a seven-time All-Star. This came despite the fact that Doby faced excessive abuse from fans, opponents, and even his own teammates.

Cleveland's Larry Doby, *right*, and Steve Gromek hug after the Indians won Game 4 of the 1948 World Series.

And, for five years, Doby could never stay at the Indians' team hotel because he was black.

SATCHEL PAIGE

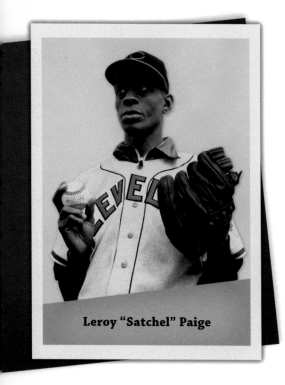

Leroy "Satchel" Paige

In the middle of the 1948 season, Negro Leagues legend Leroy "Satchel" Paige joined the Indians. People thought it was a crazy stunt by Veeck to sell tickets. The *Sporting News* criticized the move, saying Veeck had gone "too far in his quest for publicity." "To sign a hurler of Paige's age," the *Sporting News* wrote, "is to demean the standards of baseball in the big circuits."

Paige, who was 42, proved them wrong in a huge way. The Indians sold tickets, all right. Fans crammed into ballparks to watch him. And he delivered. He threw back-to-back shutouts in August. The second one came at home before a record crowd of more than 78,000. Paige finished the 1948 season with a 6–1 record and

2.48 earned-run average
(ERA).

A Miss

By the end of the 1948
season, seven blacks
had played in the major
leagues. Dan Bankhead
had joined Robinson and
the Dodgers in August
1947. He became the
first black pitcher in
the major leagues. The
St. Louis Browns, sitting
in last place and hoping
to increase attendance,
signed two Kansas City
Monarchs stars, Willard
Brown and Hank Thompson, in 1947. That turned out to be
a disaster.

The players did not help the team win games or sell tickets.
Teammates made it clear they did not want them around. One
day, Brown was sent in as a pinch-hitter. He borrowed the bat
of white teammate Jeff Heath. Brown slugged a drive to deep

THIS OLD MAN

Leroy "Satchel" Paige was a Negro
Leagues legend, but after his rookie
season in 1948, he did not have
tremendous success in the majors. Of
course, by then Paige was old enough
to be many of his teammates' father.
He played one more season with
Cleveland and then was with the
St. Louis Browns from 1951 to 1953.
He won 12 games and had 10 saves
in 1952. In 1965, Paige came out of
retirement to pitch three innings for
the Kansas City A's at age 59. His final
major league record was 28–31. He
set records as MLB's oldest rookie
(42) and oldest player (59).

center field. He flew around the bases for an inside-the-park home run. It was the first AL home run hit by a black player. No one said a word when Brown returned to the dugout. No one shook his hand. Heath took the bat that Brown had used and smashed it to pieces.

After a few weeks, Brown and Thompson went back to the Monarchs. Not all was lost, though. Thompson later returned to the major leagues and had eight productive seasons with the New York Giants. Brown never played in the majors again, but his success in the Negro Leagues earned him induction into the National Baseball Hall of Fame in 2006.

FALL OF THE NEGRO LEAGUES

As predicted by many, the integration of MLB doomed the Negro Leagues. That was never more obvious than on May 27, 1947. According to reports, as many as 8,000 black fans lined up outside the Polo Grounds that day, hours before Jackie Robinson's Dodgers were to face the New York Giants. The crowd for the game was announced at 51,780, a Polo Grounds record for a night game. Across town, two top Negro Leagues teams, the Homestead Grays and New York Black Yankees, were playing at Yankee Stadium. That game drew just 2,600 fans. In the 1950s, blacks flocked to see black major leaguers and largely ignored the Negro Leagues. By 1960, the Negro Leagues were just a memory.

From left, **Monte Irvin, Willie Mays, and Hank Thompson of the New York Giants made up MLB's first all-black outfield during the 1951 World Series.**

ROY CAMPANELLA

Perhaps the best of the early black major leaguers was another Rickey find: Roy Campanella. The barrel-chested catcher had

been a Negro Leagues star before Rickey signed him in March 1946. Campanella spent two seasons in the minors before joining the Dodgers in 1948. Over the next 10 seasons, he was an eight-time All-Star and three-time NL Most Valuable Player (MVP). In 1953, he hit .312 with 41 home runs and 142 runs batted in (RBIs). More than 50 years later, it still ranks as one of the greatest seasons ever for a catcher.

In the first two seasons with blacks

"BIG NEWK"

Leroy "Satchel" Paige had a great 1948 season with Cleveland, but the first star black pitcher in the majors was Don Newcombe. The 6-foot-4 pitcher, nicknamed "Big Newk," played 10 seasons in the majors, most of them with the Dodgers. And he missed two seasons in the 1950s while serving in the army.

Newcombe was named the NL Rookie of the Year in 1949 when he went 17–8. In 1956, Newcombe went 27–7 with an ERA of 3.06. That season he won both the NL MVP and Cy Young awards. He became the first player in baseball history to win the Rookie of the Year, MVP, and Cy Young awards. In 2011, Detroit Tigers pitcher Justin Verlander became the second to do so.

Catcher Roy Campanella was a three-time NL MVP while playing for the Brooklyn Dodgers from 1948 to 1957.

in the majors, the only integrated teams in baseball had reached the World Series. Brooklyn did so in 1947 and Cleveland a year later. For years, one of the arguments against blacks in the majors was that they did not have the skill to compete. Robinson, Doby, and Campanella clearly showed that was not true.

> **"You've got to attribute a huge piece of the Dodgers' success to black players. They didn't bring us up because we were black. They brought us up because they thought we were better than the white guy at that position. And they thought we could help the team win. And we did."**
>
> —*Don Newcombe*

The Dodgers added black pitcher Don Newcombe in 1949. He went 17–8 and was named the NL Rookie of the Year. Led by three black players— Robinson, Campanella, and Newcombe—the Dodgers reached the World Series again in 1949.

SLOW GROWTH

It seemed logical that many MLB teams would start signing the top Negro Leagues players. But that did not happen. When the 1949 season began, only Brooklyn and Cleveland had any blacks in the majors. That year, there were 36 black players in organized baseball, including the minor leagues. Twenty-six of them were in either the Dodgers' or Indians' organization.

From left: **black players Roy Campanella, Larry Doby, Don Newcombe, and Jackie Robinson played in the 1949 All-Star Game.**

Most teams preferred to remain all white well into the 1950s. Because of that, they missed out on some of the greatest players in baseball history.

5

ALL TEAMS ON BOARD

Between 1950 and 1954, the number of blacks in the majors jumped from nine to 38. But more than 10 years after Jackie Robinson joined the Brooklyn Dodgers, there were still some holdouts with no blacks on their major league rosters.

In New York, the Giants had signed their first black player, Monte Irvin, in 1949. Irvin pounded the ball in 1951, hitting .312 with 24 home runs. He led the NL with 121 RBIs.

Early that season, the Giants were struggling along in fifth place. Looking for